KARL-LUDWIG SAND

by

Alexandre Dumas

Copyright © 2012 Read Books Ltd.
This book is copyright and may not be
reproduced or copied in any way without
the express permission of the publisher in writing

British Library Cataloguing-in-Publication Data
A catalogue record for this book is available from the
British Library

Alexandre Dumas

Alexandre Dumas was born in Villers-Cotterêts, France in 1802. His parents were poor, but their heritage and good reputation – Alexandre's father had been a general in Napoleon's army – provided Alexandre with opportunities for good employment. In 1822, Dumas moved to Paris to work for future king Louis Philippe I in the Palais Royal. It was here that he began to write for magazines and the theatre.

In 1829 and 1830 respectively, Dumas produced the plays Henry III and His Court and Christine, both of which met with critical acclaim and financial success. As a result, he was able to commit himself full-time to writing. Despite the turbulent economic times which followed the Revolution of 1830, Dumas turned out to have something of an entrepreneurial streak, and did well for himself in this decade. He founded a production studio that turned out hundreds of stories under his creative direction, and began to produce serialised novels for newspapers which were widely read by the French public. It was over the next two decades, as a now famous and much loved author of romantic and adventuring sagas, that Dumas produced his best-known works – the D'Artagnan romances, including The Three Musketeers, in 1844, and The Count of Monte Cristo, in 1846.

Dumas made a lot of money from his writing, but he was almost constantly penniless as a result of his extravagant lifestyle and love of women. In 1851 he fled his creditors to Belgium, and then Russia, and then Italy, not returning to Paris until 1864. Dumas died in Puys, France, in 1870, at the age of 68. He is now enshrined in the Panthéon of Paris alongside fellow authors Victor Hugo and Emile Zola. Since his death, his fiction has been translated into almost a hundred languages, and has formed the basis for more than 200 motion pictures.

KARL-LUDWIG SAND

On the 22nd of March, 1819, about nine o'clock in the morning, a young man, some twenty-three or twenty-four years old, wearing the dress of a German student, which consists of a short frock-coat with silk braiding, tight trousers, and high boots, paused upon a little eminence that stands upon the road between Kaiserthal and Mannheim, at about three-quarters of the distance from the former town, and commands a view of the latter. Mannheim is seen rising calm and smiling amid gardens which once were ramparts, and which now surround and embrace it like a girdle of foliage and flowers. Having reached this spot, he lifted his cap, above the peak of which were embroidered three interlaced oak leaves in silver, and uncovering his brow, stood bareheaded for a moment to feel the fresh air that rose from the valley of the Neckar. At first sight his irregular features produced a strange impression; but before long the pallor of his face, deeply marked by smallpox, the infinite gentleness of his eyes, and the elegant framework of his long and flowing black hair, which grew in an admirable curve around a broad, high forehead, attracted towards him that emotion of sad sympathy to which we yield without inquiring its reason or dreaming of resistance. Though it was still early, he seemed already to have come some distance, for his boots were covered with dust; but no doubt he was nearing his destination, for, letting his cap drop, and hooking into his belt his long pipe, that inseparable companion of the German Borsch, he drew from his pocket a little note-book, and wrote in it with a pencil: "Left Wanheim at five in the morning, came in sight of Mannheim at a quarter-past nine." Then putting his note-book back into his pocket, he stood motionless for a moment, his lips moving as though in mental prayer, picked up his hat, and walked on again with a firm step towards Mannheim.

This young Student was Karl-Ludwig Sand, who was coming from Jena, by way of Frankfort aid Darmstadt, in order to assassinate Kotzebue.

Now, as we are about to set before our readers one of those terrible actions for the true appreciation of which the conscience is the sole judge, they must allow us to make them fully acquainted with him whom kings regarded as an assassin, judges as a fanatic, and the youth of Germany as a hero. Charles Louis Sand was born on the 5th of October, 1795, at Wonsiedel, in the Fichtel Wald; he was the youngest son of Godfrey Christopher Sand, first president and councillor of justice to the King of Prussia, and of Dorothea Jane Wilheltmina Schapf, his wife. Besides two elder brothers, George, who entered upon a commercial career at St, Gall, and Fritz, who was an advocate in the Berlin court of appeal, he had an elder sister named Caroline, and a younger sister called Julia.

While still in the cradle he had been attacked by smallpox of the most malignant type. The virus having spread through all his body, laid bare his ribs, and almost ate away his skull. For several months he lay between life and death; but life at last gained the upper hand. He remained weak and sickly, however, up to his seventh year, at which time a brain fever attacked him; and again put his life in danger. As a compensation, however, this fever, when it left him, seemed to carry away with it all vestiges of his former illness. From that moment his health and strength came into existence; but during these two long illnesses his education had remained very backward, and it was not until the age of eight that he could begin his elementary studies; moreover, his physical sufferings having retarded his intellectual development, he needed to work twice as hard as others to reach the same result.

Seeing the efforts that young Sand made, even while still quite a child, to conquer the defects of his organisation, Professor Salfranck, a learned and distinguished man, rector of the Hof gymnasium [college], conceived such an affection for him, that when, at a later time, he was appointed director of the gymnasium at Ratisbon, he could not part from his pupil, and took him with him. In this town, and at the age of eleven years, he gave the first proof of his courage and humanity. One day, when he was walking with some young friends, he heard cries for help, and ran in that direction: a little boy, eight or nine years old, had just fallen into a pond. Sand immediately, without regarding his best clothes, of which, however, he was very proud, sprang into the water, and, after unheard-of efforts for a child of his age, succeeded in bringing the drowning boy to land.

At the age of twelve or thirteen, Sand, who had become more active, skilful, and determined than many of his elders, often amused himself by giving battle to the lads of the town and of the neighbouring villages. The theatre of these childish conflicts, which in their pale innocence reflected the great battles that were at that time steeping Germany in blood, was generally a plain extending from the town of Wonsiedel to the mountain of St. Catherine, which had ruins at its top, and amid the ruins a tower in excellent preservation. Sand, who was one of the most eager fighters, seeing that his side had several times been defeated on account of its numerical inferiority, resolved, in order to make up for this drawback, to fortify the tower of St. Catherine, and to retire into it at the next battle if its issue proved unfavourable to him. He communicated this plan to his companions, who received it with enthusiasm. A week was spent, accordingly, in collecting all possible weapons of defence in the tower and in repairing its doors and stairs. These preparations were made so secretly that the army of the enemy had no knowledge of them.

Sunday came: the holidays were the days of battle. Whether because the boys were ashamed of having been beaten last time, or for some other reason, the band to which Sand belonged was even weaker than usual. Sure, however, of a means of retreat, he accepted battle, notwithstanding. The struggle was not a long one; the one party was too weak in numbers to make a prolonged resistance, and began to retire in the best order that could be maintained to St. Catherine's tower, which was reached before much damage had been felt. Having arrived there, some of the combatants ascended to the ramparts, and while the others defended themselves at the foot of the wall, began to shower stones and pebbles upon the conquerors. The latter, surprised at the new method of defence which was now for the first time adopted, retreated a little; the rest of the defenders took advantage of the moment to retire into the fortress and shut the door. Great was the astonishment an the part of the besiegers: they had always seen that door broken down, and lo! all at once it was presenting to them a barrier which preserved the besieged from their blows. Three or four went off to find instruments with which to break it down and meanwhile the rest of the attacking farce kept the garrison blockaded.

At the end of half an hour the messengers returned not only with levers and picks, but also with a considerable reinforcement composed of lads from, the village to which they had been to fetch tools.

Then began the assault: Sand and his companions defended themselves desperately; but it was soon evident that, unless help came, the garrison would be forced to capitulate. It was proposed that they should draw lots, and that one of the besieged should be chosen, who in spite of the danger should leave the tower, make his way as best he might through the enemy's army, and go to summon the other lads of Wonsiedel, who had faint-heartedly remained at home. The tale of the peril in which their Comrades actually were, the disgrace of a surrender, which would fall upon all of them, would no doubt overcome their indolence and induce them to make a diversion that would allow the garrison to attempt sortie. This suggestion was adopted; but instead of leaving the decision to chance, Sand proposed himself as the messenger. As everybody knew his courage, his skill, and his lightness of foot, the proposition was unanimously accepted, and the new Decius prepared to execute his act of devotion. The deed was not free from danger: there were but two means of egress, one by way of the door, which would lead to the fugitive's falling immediately into the hands of the enemy; the other by jumping from a rampart so high that the enemy had not set a guard there. Sand without a moment's hesitation went to the rampart, where, always religious, even in his childish pleasures, he made a short prayer; then, without fear, without hesitation, with a confidence that was almost superhuman, he sprang to the ground: the distance was twenty-two feet. Sand flew instantly to Wonsiedel, and reached it, although the enemy had despatched their best runners in pursuit. Then the garrison, seeing the success of their enterprise, took fresh courage, and united their efforts against the besiegers, hoping everything from Sand's eloquence, which gave him a great influence over his young companions. And, indeed, in half an hour he was seen reappearing at the head of some thirty boys of his own age, armed with slings and crossbows. The besiegers, on the point of being attacked before and behind, recognised the disadvantage of their position and retreated. The victory remained with Sand's party, and all the honours of the day were his.

We have related this anecdote in detail, that our readers may understand from the character of the child what was that of the man. Besides, we shall see him develop, always calm and superior amid small events as amid large ones.

About the same time Sand escaped almost miraculously from two dangers. One day a hod full of plaster fell from a scaffold and broke at his feet. Another day the Price of Coburg, who during the King of Prussia's stay at the baths of Alexander, was living in the house of Sand's parents, was galloping home with four horses when he came suddenly upon young Karl in a gateway; he could not escape either on the right or the left, without running the risk of being crushed between the wall and the wheels, and the coachman could not, when going at such a pace, hold in his horses: Sand flung himself on his face, and the carriage passed over him without his receiving so much as a single scratch either from the horses or the wheels. From that moment many people regarded him as predestined, and said that the hand of God was upon him.

Meanwhile political events were developing themselves around the boy, and their seriousness made him a man before the age of manhood. Napoleon weighed upon Germany like another Sennacherib. Staps had tried to play the part of Mutius Scaevola, and had died a martyr. Sand was at Hof at that time, and was a student of the gymnasium of which his good tutor Salfranck was the head. He learned that the man whom he regarded as the antichrist was to come and review the troops in that town; he left it at once and went home to his parents, who asked him for what reason he had left the gymnasium.

"Because I could not have been in the same town with

Napoleon," he answered, "without trying to kill him, and I do not feel my hand strong enough for that yet."

This happened in 1809; Sand was fourteen years old. Peace, which was signed an the 15th of October, gave Germany some respite, and allowed the young fanatic to resume his studies without being distracted by political considerations; but in 1811 he was occupied by them again, when he learned that the gymnasium was to be dissolved and its place taken by a primary school. To this the rector Salfranck was appointed as a teacher, but instead of the thousand florins which his former appointment brought him, the new one was worth only five hundred. Karl could not remain in a primary school where he could not continue his education; he wrote to his mother to announce this event and to tell her with what equanimity the old German philosopher had borne it. Here is the answer of Sand's mother; it will serve to show the character of the woman whose mighty heart never belied itself in the midst of the severest suffering; the answer bears the stamp of that German mysticism of which we have no idea in France:—

"MY DEAR KARL,—You could not have given me a more grievous piece of news than that of the event which has just fallen upon your tutor and father by adoption; nevertheless, terrible though it may be, do not doubt that he will resign himself to it, in order to give to the virtue of his pupils a great example of that submission which every subject owes to the king wham God has set over him. Furthermore, be well assured that in this world there is no other upright and well calculated policy than that which grows out of the old precept, 'Honour God, be just and fear not.' And reflect also that when injustice against the worthy becomes crying, the public voice makes itself heard, and uplifts those who are cast down.

"But if, contrary to all probability, this did not happen,—if God should impose this sublime probation upon the virtue of our friend, if the world were to disown him and Providence were to became to that, degree his debtor,—yet in that case there are, believe me, supreme compensations: all the things and all the events that occur around us and that act upon us are but machines set in motion by a Higher Hand, so as to complete our education for a higher world, in which alone we shall take our true place. Apply yourself, therefore, my dear child, to watch over yourself unceasingly and always, so that you may not take great and fine isolated actions for real virtue, and may be ready every moment to do all that your duty may require of you. Fundamentally nothing is great, you see, and nothing small, when things are, looked at apart from one another, and it is only the putting of things together that produces the unity of evil or of good.

"Moreover, God only sends the trial to the heart where He has put strength, and the manner in which you tell me that your master has borne the misfortune that has befallen him is a fresh proof of this great and eternal truth. You must form yourself upon him, my dear child, and if you are obliged to leave Hof for Bamberg you must resign yourself to it courageously. Man has three educations: that which he receives from his parents, that which circumstances impose upon him, and lastly that which he gives himself; if that misfortune should occur, pray to God that you may yourself worthily complete that last education, the most important of all.

"I will give you as an example the life and conduct of my father, of whom you have not heard very much, for he died before you were born, but whose mind and likeness are reproduced in you only among all your brothers and sisters. The disastrous fire which reduced his native town to ashes destroyed his fortune and that of his relatives; grief at having lost everything—for the fire broke out in the next house to his—cost his father his life; and while his mother, who for six years had been stretched an a bed of pain, where horrible convulsions held her fast, supported her three little girls by the needlework that she did in the intervals of suffering, he went as a mere clerk into one of the leading mercantile houses of Augsburg, where his lively and yet even temper made him welcome; there he learned a calling, for which, however, he was not naturally adapted, and came back to the home of his birth with a pure and stainless heart, in order to be the support of his mother and his sisters.

"A man can do much when he wishes to do much: join your efforts to my prayers, and leave the rest in the hands of God."

The prediction of this Puritan woman was fulfilled: a little time afterwards rector Salfranck was appointed professor at Richembourg, whither Sand followed him; it was there that the events of 1813 found him. In the month of March he wrote to his mother:—

"I can scarcely, dear mother, express to you how calm and happy I begin to feel since I am permitted to believe in the enfranchisement of my country, of which I hear on every side as being so near at hand,—of that country which, in my faith in God, I see beforehand free and mighty, that country for whose happiness I would undergo the greatest sufferings, and even death. Take strength for this crisis. If by chance it should reach our good province, lift your eyes to the Almighty, then carry them back to beautiful rich nature. The goodness of God which preserved and protected so many men during the disastrous Thirty Years' War can do and will do now what it could and did then. As for me, I believe and hope."

Leipzig came to justify Sand's presentiments; then the year 1814 arrived, and he thought Germany free.

On the 10th of December in the same year he left Richembourg with this certificate from his master:—

"Karl Sand belongs to the small number of those elect young men who are distinguished at once by the gifts of the mind and the faculties of the soul; in application and work he surpasses all his fellow-students, and this fact explains his rapid progress in all the philosophical and philological sciences; in mathematics only there are still some further studies which he might pursue. The most affectionate wishes of his teacher follow him on his departure.

"J. A. KEYN, "Rector, and master of the first class. "Richembourg, Sept. 15, 1814"

But it was really the parents of Sand, and in particular his mother, who had prepared the fertile soil in which his teachers had sowed the seeds of learning; Sand knew this well, for at the moment of setting out for the university of Tubingen, where he was about to complete the theological studies necessary for becoming a pastor, as he desired to do, he wrote to them:—

"I confess that, like all my brothers and sisters, I owe to you that beautiful and great part of my education which I have seen to be lacking to most of those around me. Heaven alone can reward you by a conviction of having so nobly and grandly fulfilled your parental duties, amid many others."

After having paid a visit to his brother at St. Gall, Sand reached Tubingen, to which he had been principally attracted by the reputation of Eschenmayer; he spent that winter quietly, and no other incident befell than his admission into an association of Burschen, called the Teutonic; then came tester of 1815, and with it the terrible news that Napoleon had landed in the Gulf of Juan. Immediately all the youth of Germany able to bear arms gathered once more around the banners of 1813 and 1814. Sand followed the general example; but the action, which in others was an effect of enthusiasm, was in him the result of calm and deliberate resolution. He wrote to Wonsiedel on this occasion:—

"April 22, 1813

"MY DEAR PARENTS,—Until now you have found me submissive to your parental lessons and to the advice of my excellent masters; until now I have made efforts to render myself worthy of the education that God has sent me through you, and have applied myself to become capable of spreading the word of the Lord through my native land; and for this reason I can to-day declare to you sincerely the decision that I lave taken, assured that as tender and affectionate parents you will calm yourselves, and as German parents and patriots you will rather praise my resolution than seek to turn me from it.

"The country calls once more for help, and this time the call is addressed to me, too, for now I have courage and strength. It cast me a great in ward struggle, believe me, to abstain when in 1813 she gave her first cry, and only the conviction held me back that thousands of others were then fighting and conquering for Germany, while I had to live far the peaceful calling to which I was destined. Now it is a question of preserving our newly re-established liberty, which in so many places has already brought in so rich a harvest. The all-powerful and merciful Lord reserves for us this great trial, which will certainly be the last; it is for us, therefore, to show that we are worthy of the supreme gift which He has given us, and capable of upholding it with strength and firmness.

"The danger of the country has never been so great as it is now, that is why, among the youth of Germany, the strong should support the wavering, that all may rise together. Our brave brothers in the north are already assembling from all parts under their banners; the State of Wurtemburg is, proclaiming a general levy, and volunteers are coming in from every quarter, asking to die for their country. I consider it my duty, too, to fight for my country and for all the dear ones whom I love. If I were not profoundly convinced of this truth, I should not communicate my resolution to you; but my family is one that has a really German heart, and that would consider me as a coward and an unworthy son if I did not follow this impulse. I certainly feel the greatness of the sacrifice; it costs me something, believe me, to leave my beautiful studies and go to put myself under the orders of vulgar, uneducated people, but this only increases my courage in going to secure the liberty of my brothers; moreover, when once that liberty is secured, if God deigns to allow, I will return to carry them His word.

"I take leave, therefore, for a time of you, my most worthy parents, of my brothers, my sisters, and all who are dear to me. As, after mature deliberation, it seems the most suitable thing for me to serve with the Bavarians. I shall get myself enrolled, for as long as the war may last, with a company of that nation. Farewell, then; live happily; far away from you as I shall be, I shall follow your pious exhortations. In this new track I shall still I hope, remain pure before God, and I shall always try to walk in the path that rises above the things of earth and leads to those of heaven, and perhaps in this career the bliss of saving some souls from their fall may be reserved for me.

"Your dear image will always be about me; I will always have the Lord before my eyes and in my heart, so that I may endure joyfully the pains and fatigues of this holy war. Include me in your Prayers; God will send you the hope of better times to help you in bearing the unhappy time in which we now are. We cannot see one another again soon, unless we conquer; and if we should be conquered (which God forbid!), then my last wish, which I pray you, I conjure you, to fulfil, my last and supreme wish would be that you, my dear and deserving German relatives, should leave an enslaved country for some other not yet under the yoke.

"But why should we thus sadden one another's hearts? Is not our cause just and holy, and is not God just and holy? How then should we not be victors? You see that sometimes I doubt, so, in your letters, which I am impatiently expecting, have pity on me and do not alarm my soul, far in any case we shall meet again in another country, and that one will always be free and happy.

"I am, until death, your dutiful and grateful son, "KARL SAND."

These two lines of Korner's were written as a postscript:
"Perchance above our foeman lying dead
  We may behold the star of liberty."

With this farewell to his parents, and with Korner's poems on his lips, Sand gave up his books, and on the 10th of May we find him in arms among the volunteer chasseurs enrolled under the command of Major Falkenhausen, who was at that time at Mannheim; here he found his second brother, who had preceded him, and they underwent all their drill together.

Though Sand was not accustomed to great bodily fatigues, he endured those of the campaign with surprising strength, refusing all the alleviations that his superiors tried to offer him; for he would allow no one to outdo him in the trouble that he took for the good of the country. On the march he invariably shared: anything that he possessed fraternally with his comrades, helping those who were weaker than himself to carry their burdens, and, at once priest and soldier, sustaining them by his words when he was powerless to do anything more.

On the 18th of June, at eight o'clock in the evening, he arrived upon the field of battle at Waterloo, On the 14th of July he entered Paris.

On the 18th of December, 1815, Karl Sand and his brother were back at Wonsiedel, to the great joy of their family. He spent the Christmas holidays and the end of the year with them, but his ardour for his new vacation did not allow him to remain longer, and an the 7th of January he reached Erlangen. Then, to make up for lost time, he resolved to subject his day to fixed and uniform rules, and to write down every evening what he had done since the morning. It is by the help of this journal that we are able to follow the young enthusiast, not only in all the actions of his life, but also in all the thoughts of his mind and all the hesitations of his conscience. In it we find his whole self, simple to naivete, enthusiastic to madness, gentle even to weakness towards others, severe even to asceticism towards himself. One of his great griefs was the expense that his education occasioned to his parents, and every useless and costly pleasure left a remorse in his heart. Thus, on the 9th of February 1816, he wrote:—

"I meant to go and visit my parents. Accordingly I went to the 'Commers-haus', and there I was much amused. N. and T. began upon me with the everlasting jokes about Wonsiedel; that went on until eleven o'clock. But afterwards N. and T. began to torment me to go to the wine-shop; I refused as long as I could. But as, at last, they seemed to think that it was from contempt of them that I would not go and drink a glass of Rhine wine with them, I did not dare resist longer. Unfortunately, they did not stop at Braunberger; and while my glass was still half full, N. ordered a bottle of champagne. When the first had disappeared, T. ordered a second; then, even before this second battle was drunk, both of them ordered a third in my name and in spite of me. I returned home quite giddy, and threw myself on the sofa, where I slept for about an hour, and only went to bed afterwards.

"Thus passed this shameful day, in which I have not thought enough of my kind and worthy parents, who are leading a poor and hard life, and in which I suffered myself to be led away by the example of people who have money into spending four florins—an expenditure which was useless, and which would have kept the whole family for two days. Pardon me, my God, pardon me, I beseech Thee, and receive the vow that I make never to fall into the same fault again. In future I will live even more abstemiously than I usually do, so as to repair the fatal traces in my poor cashbox of my extravagance, and not to be obliged to ask money of my mother before the day when she thinks of sending me some herself."

Then, at the very time when the poor young man reproaches himself as if with a crime with having spent four florins, one of his cousins, a widow, dies and leaves three orphan children. He runs immediately to carry the first consolations to the unhappy little creatures, entreats his mother to take charge of the youngest, and overjoyed at her answer, thanks her thus:—

"Far the very keen joy that you have given me by your letter, and for the very dear tone in which your soul speaks to me, bless you, O my mother! As I might have hoped and been sure, you have taken little Julius, and that fills me afresh with the deepest gratitude towards you, the rather that, in my constant trust in your goodness, I had already in her lifetime given our good little cousin the promise that you are fulfilling for me after her death."

About March, Sand, though he did not fall ill, had an indisposition that obliged him to go and take the waters; his mother happened at the time to be at the ironworks of Redwitz, same twelve or fifteen miles from Wonsiedel, where the mineral springs are found. Sand established himself there with his mother, and notwithstanding his desire to avoid interrupting his work, the time taken up by baths, by invitations to dinners, and even by the walks which his health required, disturbed the regularity of his usual existence and awakened his remorse. Thus we find these lines written in his journal for April 13th:

"Life, without some high aim towards which all thoughts and actions tend, is an empty desert: my day yesterday is a proof of this; I spent it with my own people, and that, of course, was a great pleasure to me; but how did I spend it? In continual eating, so that when I wanted to work I could do nothing worth doing. Full of indolence and slackness, I dragged myself into the company of two or three sets of people, and came from them in the same state of mind as I went to them."

Far these expeditions Sand made use of a little chestnut horse which belonged to his brother, and of which he was very fond. This little horse had been bought with great difficulty; for, as we have said, the whole family was poor. The following note, in relation to the animal, will give an idea of Sand's simplicity of heart:—

"19th April "To-day I have been very happy at the ironworks, and very industrious beside my kind mother. In the evening I came home on the little chestnut. Since the day before yesterday, when he got a strain and hurt his foot, he has been very restive and very touchy, and when he got home he refused his food. I thought at first that he did not fancy his fodder, and gave him some pieces of sugar and sticks of cinnamon, which he likes very much; he tasted them, but would not eat them. The poor little beast seems to have same other internal indisposition besides his injured foot. If by ill luck he were to become foundered or ill, everybody, even my parents, would throw the blame on me, and yet I have been very careful and considerate of him. My God, my Lord, Thou who canst do things both great and small, remove from me this misfortune, and let him recover as quickly as possible. If, however, Thou host willed otherwise, and if this fresh trouble is to fall upon us, I will try to bear it with courage, and as the expiation of same sin. Meanwhile, O my Gad, I leave this matter in Thy hands, as I leave my life and my soul."

On the 20th of April he wrote:—"The little horse is well; God has helped me."

German manners and customs are so different from ours, and contrasts occur so frequently in the same man, on the other side of the Rhine, that anything less than all the quotations which we have given would have been insufficient to place before our readers a true idea of that character made up of artlessness and reason, childishness and strength, depression and enthusiasm, material details and poetic ideas, which renders Sand a man incomprehensible to us. We will now continue the portrait, which still wants a few finishing touches.

When he returned to Erlangen, after the completion of his "cure," Sand read Faust far the first time. At first he was amazed at that work, which seemed to him an orgy of genius; then, when he had entirely finished it, he reconsidered his first impression, and wrote:—

"4th May

"Oh, horrible struggle of man and devil! What Mephistopheles is in me I feel far the first time in this hour, and I feel it, O God, with consternation!

"About eleven at night I finished reading the tragedy, and I felt and saw the fiend in myself, so that by midnight, amid my tears and despair, I was at last frightened at myself."

Sand was falling by degrees into a deep melancholy, from which nothing could rouse him except his desire to purify and preach morality to the students around him. To anyone who knows university life such a task will seem superhuman. Sand, however, was not discouraged, and if he could not gain an influence over everyone, he at least succeeded in forming around him a considerable circle of the most intelligent and the best; nevertheless, in the midst of these apostolic labours strange longings for death would overcome him; he seemed to recall heaven and want to return to it; he called these temptations "homesickness for the soul's country."

His favourite authors were Lessing, Schiller, Herder, and Goethe; after re-reading the two last for the twentieth time, this is what he wrote:

"Good and evil touch each other; the woes of the young Werther and Weisslingen's seduction, are almost the same story; no matter, we must not judge between what is good and what is evil in others; for that is what God will do. I have just been spending much time over this thought, and have become convinced that in no circumstances ought we to allow ourselves to seek for the devil in others, and that we have no right to judge; the only creature over wham we have received the power to judge and condemn is ourself, and that gives us enough constant care, business, and trouble.

"I have again to-day felt a profound desire to quit this world and enter a higher world; but this desire is rather dejection than strength, a lassitude than an upsoaring."

The year 1816 was spent by Sand in these pious attempts

upon his young comrades, in this ceaseless self-examination, and in the perpetual battle which he waged with the desire for death that pursued him; every day he had deeper doubts of himself; and on the 1st of January, 1817, he wrote this prayer in his diary:—

"Grant to me, O Lord, to me whom Thou halt endowed, in sending me on earth, with free will, the grace that in this year which we are now beginning I may never relax this constant attention, and not shamefully give up the examination of my conscience which I have hitherto made. Give me strength to increase the attention which I turn upon my own life, and to diminish that which I turn upon the life of others; strengthen my will that it may become powerful to command the desires of the body and the waverings of the soul; give me a pious conscience entirely devoted to Thy celestial kingdom, that I may always belong to Thee, or after failing, may be able to return to Thee."

Sand was right in praying to God for the year 1817, and his fears were a presentiment: the skies of Germany, lightened by Leipzig and Waterloo, were once more darkened; to the colossal and universal despotism of Napoleon succeeded the individual oppression of those little princes who made up the Germanic Diet, and all that the nations had gained by overthrowing the giant was to be governed by dwarfs. This was the time when secret societies were organised throughout Germany; let us say a few words about them, for the history that we are writing is not only that of individuals, but also that of nations, and every time that occasion presents itself we will give our little picture a wide horizon.

The secret societies of Germany, of which, without knowing them, we have all heard, seem, when we follow them up, like rivers, to originate in some sort of affiliation to those famous clubs of the 'illumines' and the freemasons which made so much stir in France at the close of the eighteenth century. At the time of the revolution of '89 these different philosophical, political, and religious sects enthusiastically accepted the republican doctrines, and the successes of our first generals have often been attributed to the secret efforts of the members. When Bonaparte, who was acquainted with these groups, and was even said to have belonged to them, exchanged his general's uniform for an emperor's cloak, all of them, considering him as a renegade and traitor, not only rose against him at home, but tried to raise enemies against him abroad; as they addressed themselves to noble and generous passions, they found a response, and princes to whom their results might be profitable seemed for a moment to encourage them. Among others, Prince Louis of Prussia was grandmaster of one of these societies.

The attempted murder by Stops, to which we have already referred, was one of the thunderclaps of the storm; but its morrow brought the peace of Vienna, and the degradation of Austria was the death-blow of the old Germanic organisation. These societies, which had received a mortal wound in 1806 and were now controlled by the French police, instead of continuing to meet in public, were forced to seek new members in the dark. In 1811 several agents of these societies were arrested in Berlin, but the Prussian authorities, following secret orders of Queen Louisa, actually protected them, so that they were easily able to deceive the French police about their intentions. About February 1815 the disasters of the French army revived the courage of these societies, for it was seen that God was helping their cause: the students in particular joined enthusiastically in the new attempts that were now begun; many colleges enrolled themselves almost entire, anal chose their principals and professors as captains; the poet, Korner, killed on the 18th of October at Liegzig, was the hero of this campaign.

The triumph of this national movement, which twice carried the Prussian army—largely composed of volunteers—to Paris, was followed, when the treaties of 1815 and the new Germanic constitution were made known, by a terrible reaction in Germany. All these young men who, exiled by their princes, had risen in the name of liberty, soon perceived that they had been used as tools to establish European despotism; they wished to claim the promises that had been made, but the policy of Talleyrand and Metternich weighed on them, and repressing them at the first words they uttered, compelled them to shelter their discontent and their hopes in the universities, which, enjoying a kind of constitution of their own, more easily escaped the investigations made by the spies of the Holy Alliance; but, repressed as they were, these societies continued nevertheless to exist, and kept up communications by means of travelling students, who, bearing verbal messages, traversed Germany under the pretence of botanising, and, passing from mountain to mountain, sowed broadcast those luminous and hopeful words of which peoples are always greedy and kings always fear.

We have seen that Sand, carried away by the general movement, had gone through the campaign of 1815 as a volunteer, although he was then only nineteen years old. On his return, he, like others, had found his golden hopes deceived, and it is from this period that we find his journal assuming the tone of mysticism and sadness which our readers must have remarked in it. He soon entered one of these associations, the Teutonia; and from that moment, regarding the great cause which he had taken up as a religious one, he attempted to make the conspirators worthy of their enterprise, and thus arose his attempts to inculcate moral doctrines, in which he succeeded with some, but failed with the majority. Sand had succeeded, however, in forming around him a certain circle of Puritans, composed of about sixty to eighty students, all belonging to the group of the 'Burschenschaft' which continued its political and religious course despite all the jeers of the opposing group—the 'Landmannschaft'. One of his friends called Dittmar and he were pretty much the chiefs, and although no election had given them their authority, they exercised so much influence upon what was decided that in any particular case their fellow-adepts were sure spontaneously to obey any impulse that they might choose to impart. The meetings of the Burschen took place upon a little hill crowned by a ruined castle, which was situated at some distance from Erlangen, and which Sand and Dittmar had called the Ruttli, in memory of the spot where Walter Furst, Melchthal, and Stauffacher had made their vow to deliver their country; there, under the pretence of students' games, while they built up a new house with the ruined fragments, they passed alternately from symbol to action and from action to symbol.

Meanwhile the association was making such advances throughout Germany that not only the princes and kings of the German confederation, but also the great European powers, began to be uneasy. France sent agents to bring home reports, Russia paid agents on the spot, and the persecutions that touched a professor and exasperated a whole university often arose from a note sent by the Cabinet of the Tuileries or of St. Petersburg.

It was amid the events that began thus that Sand, after commending himself to the protection of God, began the year 1817, in the sad mood in which we have just seen him, and in which he was kept rather by a disgust for things as they were than by a disgust for life. On the 8th of May, preyed upon by this melancholy, which he cannot conquer, and which comes from the disappointment of all his political hopes, he writes in his diary:

"I shall find it impassible to set seriously to work, and this idle temper, this humour of hypochondria which casts its black veil over everything in life,—continues and grows in spite of the moral activity which I imposed on myself yesterday."

In the holidays, fearing to burden his parents with any

additional expense, he will not go home, and prefers to make a walking tour with his friends. No doubt this tour, in addition to its recreative side, had a political aim. Be that as it may, Sand's diary, during the period of his journey, shows nothing but the names of the towns through which he passed. That we may have a notion of Sand's dutifulness to his parents, it should be said that he did not set out until he had obtained his mother's permission. On their return, Sand, Dittmar, and their friends the Burschen, found their Ruttli sacked by their enemies of the Landmannschaft; the house that they had built was demolished and its fragments dispersed. Sand took this event for an omen, and was greatly depressed by it.

"It seems to me, O my God!" he says in his journal, "that everything swims and turns around me. My soul grows darker and darker; my moral strength grows less instead of greater; I work and cannot achieve; walk towards my aim and do not reach it; exhaust myself, and do nothing great. The days of life flee one after another; cares and uneasiness increase; I see no haven anywhere for our sacred German cause. The end will be that we shall fall, for I myself waver. O Lord and Father! protect me, save me, and lead me to that land from which we are for ever driven back by the indifference of wavering spirits."

About this time a terrible event struck Sand to the heart; his friend Dittmar was drowned. This is what he wrote in his diary on the very morning of the occurrence:

"Oh, almighty God! What is going to become of me? For the last fortnight I have been drawn into disorder, and have not been able to compel myself to look fixedly either backward or forward in my life, so that from the 4th of June up to the present hour my journal has remained empty. Yet every day I might have had occasion to praise Thee, O my God, but my soul is in anguish. Lord, do not turn from me; the more are the obstacles the more need is there of strength."

In the evening he added these few words to the lines that he had written in the morning:—

"Desolation, despair, and death over my friend, over my very deeply loved Dittmar."

This letter which he wrote to his family contains the account of the tragic event:—

"You know that when my best friends, A., C., and Z., were gone, I became particularly intimate with my well-beloved Dittmar of Anspach; Dittmar, that is to say a true and worthy German, an evangelical Christian, something more, in short, than a man! An angelic soul, always turned toward the good, serene, pious, and ready for action; he had come to live in a room next to mine in Professor Grunler's house; we loved each other, upheld each other in our efforts, and, well or ill, bare our good or evil fortune in common. On this last spring evening, after having worked in his room and having strengthened ourselves anew to resist all the torments of life and to advance towards the aim that we desired to attain; we went, about seven in the evening, to the baths of Redwitz. A very black storm was rising in the sky, but only as yet appeared on the horizon. E., who was with us, proposed to go home, but Dittmar persisted, saying that the canal was but a few steps away. God permitted that it should not be I who replied with these fatal words. So he went on. The sunset was splendid: I see it still; its violet clouds all fringed with gold, for I remember the smallest details of that evening.

"Dittmar went down first; he was the only one of us who knew how to swim; so he walked before us to show us the depth. The water was about up to our chests, and he, who preceded us, was up to his shoulders, when he warned us not to go farther, because he was ceasing to feel the bottom. He immediately gave up his footing and began to swim, but scarcely had he made ten strokes when, having reached the place where the river separates into two branches, he uttered a cry, and as he was trying to get a foothold, disappeared. We ran at once to the bank, hoping to be able to help him more easily; but we had neither poles nor ropes within reach, and, as I have told you, neither of us could swim. Then we called for help with all our might. At that moment Dittmar reappeared, and by an unheard-of effort seized the end of a willow branch that was hanging over the water; but the branch was not strong enough to resist, and our friend sank again, as though he had been struck by apoplexy. Can you imagine the state in which we were, we his friends, bending over the river, our fixed and haggard eyes trying to pierce its depth? My God, my God! how was it we did not go mad?

"A great crowd, however, had run at our cries. For two hours they sought far him with boats and drag-hooks; and at last they succeeded in drawing his body from the gulf. Yesterday we bore it solemnly to the field of rest.

"Thus with the end of this spring has begun the serious summer of my life. I greeted it in a grave and melancholy mood, and you behold me now, if not consoled, at least strengthened by religion, which, thanks to the merits of Christ, gives me the assurance of meeting my friend in heaven, from the heights of which he will inspire me with strength to support the trials of this life; and now I do not desire anything more except to know you free from all anxiety in regard to me."

Instead of serving to unite the two groups of students in a common grief, this accident, on the contrary, did but intensify their hatred of each other. Among the first persons who ran up at the cries of Sand and his companion was a member of the Landmannschaft who could swim, but instead of going to Dittmar's assistance he exclaimed, "It seems that we shall get rid of one of these dogs of Burschen; thank God!" Notwithstanding this manifestation of hatred, which, indeed, might be that of an individual and not of the whole body, the Burschen invited their enemies to be present at Dittmar's funeral. A brutal refusal, and a threat to disturb the ceremony by insults to the corpse, formed their sole reply. The Burschen then warned the authorities, who took suitable measures, and all Dittmar's friends followed his coffin sword in hand. Beholding this calm but resolute demonstration, the Landmannschaft did not dare to carry out their threat, and contented themselves with insulting the procession by laughs and songs.

Sand wrote in his journal:

"Dittmar is a great loss to all of us, and particularly to me; he gave me the overflow of his strength and life; he stopped, as it were, with an embankment, the part of my character that is irresolute and undecided. From him it is that I have learned not to dread the approaching storm, and to know how to fight and die."

Some days after the funeral Sand had a quarrel about Dittmar with one of his former friends, who had passed over from the Burschen to the Landmannschaft, and who had made himself conspicuous at the time of the funeral by his indecent hilarity. It was decided that they should fight the next day, and on the same day Sand wrote in his journal.

"To-morrow I am to fight with P. G.; yet Thou knowest, O my God, what great friends we formerly were, except for a certain mistrust with which his coldness always inspired me; but on this occasion his odious conduct has caused me to descend from the tenderest pity to the profoundest hatred.

"My God, do not withdraw Thy hand either from him or from me, since we are both fighting like men! Judge only by our two causes, and give the victory to that which is the more just. If Thou shouldst call me before Thy supreme tribunal, I know very well that I should appear burdened with an eternal malediction; and indeed it is not upon myself that I reckon but upon the merits of our Saviour Jesus Christ.

"Come what may, be praised and blessed, O my God!

"My dear parents, brothers, and friends, I commend you to the protection of God."

Sand waited in vain for two hours next day: his adversary

did not come to the meeting place.

The loss of Dittmar, however, by no means produced the result upon Sand that might have been expected, and that he himself seems to indicate in the regrets he expressed for him. Deprived of that strong soul upon which he rested, Sand understood that it was his task by redoubled energy to make the death of Dittmar less fatal to his party. And indeed he continued singly the work of drawing in recruits which they had been carrying on together, and the patriotic conspiracy was not for a moment impeded.

The holidays came, and Sand left Erlangen to return no more. From Wonsiedel he was to proceed to Jena, in order to complete his theological studies there. After some days spent with his family, and indicated in his journal as happy, Sand went to his new place of abode, where he arrived some time before the festival of the Wartburg. This festival, established to celebrate the anniversary of the battle of Leipzig, was regarded as a solemnity throughout Germany, and although the princes well knew that it was a centre for the annual renewal of affiliation to the various societies, they dared not forbid it. Indeed, the manifesto of the Teutonic Association was exhibited at this festival and signed by more than two thousand deputies from different universities in Germany. This was a day of joy for Sand; for he found in the midst of new friends a great number of old ones.

The Government, however, which had not 'dared to attack the Association by force, resolved to undermine it by opinion. M. de Stauren published a terrible document, attacking the societies, and founded, it was said, upon information furnished by Kotzebue. This publication made a great stir, not only at Jena, but throughout all Germany. Here is the trace of this event that we find in Sand's journal:—

24th November "Today, after working with much ease and assiduity, I went out about four with E. As we crossed the market-place we heard Kotzebue's new and venomous insult read. By what a fury that man is possessed against the Burschen and against all who love Germany!"

Thus far the first time and in these terms Sand's journal presents the name of the man who, eighteen months later, he was to slay.

The Government, however, which had not 'dared to attack the Association by force, resolved to undermine it by opinion. M. de Stauren published a terrible document, attacking the societies, and founded, it was said, upon information furnished by Kotzebue. This publication made a great stir, not only at Jena, but throughout all Germany. Here is the trace of this event that we find in Sand's journal:

24th November

"To-day, after working with much ease and assiduity, I went out about four with E. As we crossed the market-place we heard Kotzebue's new and venomous insult read. By what a fury that man is possessed against the Burschen and against all who love Germany!"

Thus for the first time and in these terms Sand's journal presents the name of the man who, eighteen months later, he was to slay.

On the 29th, in the evening, Sand writes again:

"To-morrow I shall set out courageously and joyfully from this place for a pilgrimage to Wonsiedel; there I shall find my large-hearted mother and my tender sister Julia; there I shall cool my head and warm my heart. Probably I shall be present at my good Fritz's marriage with Louisa, and at the baptism of my very dear Durchmith's first-born. God, O my Father, as Thou hast been with me during my sad course, be with me still on my happy road."

This journey did in fact greatly cheer Sand. Since Dittmar's death his attacks of hypochondria had disappeared. While Dittmar lived he might die; Dittmar being dead, it was his part to live.

On the 11th of December he left Wonsiedel, to return to Jena, and on the 31st of the same month he wrote this prayer in his journal.

"O merciful Saviour! I began this year with prayer, and in these last days I have been subject to distraction and ill-disposed. When I look backward, I find, alas! that I have not become better; but I have entered more profoundly into life, and, should occasion present, I now feel strength to act.

"It is because Thou hast always been with me, Lord, even when I was not with Thee."

If our readers have followed with some attention the different extracts from the journal that we have placed before them, they must have seen Sand's resolution gradually growing stronger and his brain becoming excited. From the beginning of the year 1818, one feels his view, which long was timid and wandering, taking in a wider horizon and fixing itself on a nobler aim. He is no longer ambitious of the pastor's simple life or of the narrow influence which he might gain in a little community, and which, in his juvenile modesty, had seemed the height of good fortune and happiness; it is now his native land, his German people, nay, all humanity, which he embraces in his gigantic plans of political regeneration. Thus, on the flyleaf of his journal for the year 1818, he writes:

"Lord, let me strengthen myself in the idea that I have conceived of the deliverance of humanity by the holy sacrifice of Thy Son. Grant that I may be a Christ of Germany, and that, like and through Jesus, I may be strong and patient in suffering."

But the anti-republican pamphlets of Kotzebue increased in number and gained a fatal influence upon the minds of rulers. Nearly all the persons who were attacked in these pamphlets were known and esteemed at Jena; and it may easily be comprehended what effects were produced by such insults upon these young heads and noble hearts, which carried conviction to the paint of blindness and enthusiasm to that of fanaticism.

Thus, here is what Sand wrote in his diary on the 5th of May.

"Lord, what causes this melancholy anguish which has again taken possession of me? But a firm and constant will surmounts everything, and the idea of the country gives joy and courage to the saddest and the weakest. When I think of that, I am always amazed that there is none among us found courageous enough to drive a knife into the breast of Kotzebue or of any other traitor."

Still dominated by the same thought, he continues thus on the 18th of May:—

"A man is nothing in comparison with a nation; he is a unity compared with millions, a minute compared with a century. A man, whom nothing precedes and nothing follows, is born, lives, and dies in a longer or shorter time, which, relatively to eternity, hardly equals the duration of a lightning flash. A nation, on the contrary, is immortal."

From time to time, however, amid these thoughts that bear the impress of that political fatality which was driving him towards the deed of bloodshed, the kindly and joyous youth reappears. On the 24th of June he writes to his mother:—

"I have received your long and beautiful letter, accompanied by the very complete and well-chosen outfit which you send me. The sight of this fine linen gave me back one of the joys of my childhood. These are fresh benefits. My prayers never remain unfulfilled, and I have continual cause to thank you and God. I receive, all at once, shirts, two pairs of fine sheets, a present of your work, and of Julia's and Caroline's work, dainties and sweetmeats, so that I am still jumping with joy and I turned three times on my heels when I opened the little parcel. Receive the thanks of my heart, and share, as giver, in the joy of him who has received.

"Today, however, is a very serious day, the last day of spring and the anniversary of that on which I lost my noble and good Dittmar. I am a prey to a thousand different and confused feelings; but I have only two passions left in me which remain upright and like two pillars of brass support this whole chaos—the thought of God and the love of my country."

During all this time Sand's life remains apparently calm and equal; the inward storm is calmed; he rejoices in his application to work and his cheerful temper. However, from time to time, he makes great complaints to himself of his propensity to love dainty food, which he does not always find it possible to conquer. Then, in his self-contempt, he calls himself "fig-stomach" or "cake-stomach." But amid all this the religious and political exaltation and visits all the battlefields near to the road that he follows. On the 18th of October he is back at Jena, where he resumes his studies with more application than ever. It is among such university studies that the year 1818 closes far him, and we should hardly suspect the terrible resolution which he has taken, were it not that we find in his journal this last note, dated the 31st of December:

"I finish the last day of this year 1818, then, in a serious and solemn mood, and I have decided that the Christmas feast which has just gone by will be the last Christmas feast that I shall celebrate. If anything is to come of our efforts, if the cause of humanity is to assume the upper hand in our country, if in this faithless epoch any noble feelings can spring up afresh and make way, it can only happen if the wretch, the traitor, the seducer of youth, the infamous Kotzebue, falls! I am fully convinced of this, and until I have accomplished the work upon which I have resolved, I shall have no rest. Lord, Thou who knowest that I have devoted my life to this great action, I only need, now that it is fixed in my mind, to beg of Thee true firmness and courage of soul."

Here Sand's diary ends; he had begun it to strengthen himself; he had reached his aim; he needed nothing more. From this moment he was occupied by nothing but this single idea, and he continued slowly to mature the plan in his head in order to familiarise himself with its execution; but all the impressions arising from this thought remained in his own mind, and none was manifested on the surface. To everyone else he was the same; but for some little time past, a complete and unaltered serenity, accompanied by a visible and cheerful return of inclination towards life, had been noticed in him. He had made no charge in the hours or the duration of his studies; but he had begun to attend the anatomical classes very assiduously. One day he was seen to give even more than his customary attention to a lesson in which the professor was demonstrating the various functions of the heart; he examined with the greatest care the place occupied by it in the chest, asking to have some of the demonstrations repeated two or three times, and when he went out, questioning some of the young men who were following the medical courses, about the susceptibility of the organ, which cannot receive ever so slight a blow without death ensuing from that blow: all this with so perfect an indifference and calmness that no one about him conceived any suspicion.

Another day, A. S., one of his friends, came into his room. Sand, who had heard him coming up, was standing by the table, with a paper-knife in his hand, waiting for him; directly the visitor came in, Sand flung himself upon him, struck him lightly on the forehead; and then, as he put up his hands to ward off the blow, struck him rather more violently in the chest; then, satisfied with this experiment, said:—

"You see, when you want to kill a man, that is the way to do it; you threaten the face, he puts up his hands, and while he does so you thrust a dagger into his heart."

The two young men laughed heartily over this murderous demonstration, and A. S. related it that evening at the wine-shop as one of the peculiarities of character that were common in his friend. After the event, the pantomime explained itself.

The month of March arrived. Sand became day by day calmer, more affectionate, and kinder; it might be thought that in the moment of leaving his friends for ever he wished to leave them an ineffaceable remembrance of him. At last he announced that on account of several family affairs he was about to undertake a little journey, and set about all his preparations with his usual care, but with a serenity never previously seen in him. Up to that time he had continued to work as usual, not relaxing for an instant; for there was a possibility that Kotzebue might die or be killed by somebody else before the term that Sand had fixed to himself, and in that case he did not wish to have lost time. On the 7th of March he invited all his friends to spend the evening with him, and announced his departure for the next day but one, the 9th. All of them then proposed to him to escort him for some leagues, but Sand refused; he feared lest this demonstration, innocent though it were, might compromise them later on. He set forth alone, therefore, after having hired his lodgings for another half-year, in order to obviate any suspicion, and went by way of Erfurt and Eisenach, in order to visit the Wartburg. From that place he went to Frankfort, where he slept on the 17th, and on the morrow he continued his journey by way of Darmstadt. At last, on the 23rd, at nine in the morning, he arrived at the top of the little hill where we found him at the beginning of this narrative. Throughout the journey he had been the amiable and happy young man whom no one could see without liking.

Having reached Mannheim, he took a room at the Weinberg, and wrote his name as "Henry" in the visitors' list. He immediately inquired where Kotzebue lived. The councillor dwelt near the church of the Jesuits; his house was at the corner of a street, and though Sand's informants could not tell him exactly the letter, they assured him it was not possible to mistake the house. [At Mannheim houses are marked by letters, not by numbers.]

Sand went at once to Kotzebue's house: it was about ten o'clock; he was told that the councillor went to walk for an hour or two every morning in the park of Mannheim. Sand inquired about the path in which he generally walked, and about the clothes he wore, for never having seen him he could only recognise him by the description. Kotzebue chanced to take another path. Sand walked about the park for an hour, but seeing no one who corresponded to the description given him, went back to the house.

Kotzebue had come in, but was at breakfast and could not see him.

Sand went back to the Weinberg, and sat down to the midday table d'hote, where he dined with an appearance of such calmness, and even of such happiness, that his conversation, which was now lively, now simple, and now dignified, was remarked by everybody. At five in the afternoon he returned a third time to the house of Kotzebue, who was giving a great dinner that day; but orders had been given to admit Sand. He was shown into a little room opening out of the anteroom, and a moment after, Kotzebue came in.

Sand then performed the drama which he had rehearsed upon his friend A. S. Kotzebue, finding his face threatened, put his hands up to it, and left his breast exposed; Sand at once stabbed him to the heart; Kotzebue gave one cry, staggered, and fell back into an arm-chair: he was dead.

At the cry a little girl of six years old ran in, one of those charming German children, with the faces of cherubs, blue-eyed, with long flowing hair. She flung herself upon the body of Kotzebue, calling her father with piercing cries. Sand, standing at the door, could not endure this sight, and without going farther, he thrust the dagger, still covered with Kotzebue's blood, up to the hilt into his own breast. Then, seeing to his surprise that notwithstanding the terrible wound—he had just given himself he did not feel the approach of death, and not wishing to fall alive into the hands of the servants who were running in, he rushed to the staircase. The persons who were invited were just coming in; they, seeing a young man, pale and bleeding with a knife in his breast, uttered loud cries, and stood aside, instead of stopping him. Sand therefore passed down the staircase and reached the street below; ten paces off, a patrol was passing, on the way to relieve the sentinels at the castle; Sand thought these men had been summoned by the cries that followed him; he threw himself on his knees in the middle of the street, and said, "Father, receive my soul!"

Then, drawing the knife from the wound, he gave himself a second blow below the former, and fell insensible.

Sand was carried to the hospital and guarded with the utmost strictness; the wounds were serious, but, thanks to the skill of the physicians who were called in, were not mortal; one of them even healed eventually; but as to the second, the blade having gone between the costal pleura and the pulmonary pleura, an effusion of blood occurred between the two layers, so that, instead of closing the wound, it was kept carefully open, in order that the blood extravasated during the night might be drawn off every morning by means of a pump, as is done in the operation for empyaemia.

Notwithstanding these cares, Sand was for three months between life and death.

When, on the 26th of March, the news of Kotzebue's assassination came from Mannheim to Jena, the academic senate caused Sand's room to be opened, and found two letters—one addressed to his friends of the Burschenschaft, in which he declared that he no longer belonged to their society, since he did not wish that their brotherhood should include a man about to die an the scaffold. The other letter, which bore this superscription, "To my nearest and dearest," was an exact account of what he meant to do, and the motives which had made him determine upon this act. Though the letter is a little long, it is so solemn and so antique in spirit, that we do not hesitate to present it in its entirety to our readers:—

"To all my own "Loyal and eternally cherished souls

"Why add still further to your sadness? I asked myself, and I hesitated to write to you; but my silence would have wounded the religion of the heart; and the deeper a grief the more it needs, before it can be blotted out, to drain to the dregs its cup of bitterness. Forth from my agonised breast, then; forth, long and cruel torment of a last conversation, which alone, however, when sincere, can alleviate the pain of parting.

"This letter brings you the last farewell of your son and your brother.

"The greatest misfortune of life far any generous heart is to see the cause of God stopped short in its developments by our fault; and the most dishonouring infamy would be to suffer that the fine things acquired bravely by thousands of men, and far which thousands of men have joyfully sacrificed themselves, should be no more than a transient dream, without real and positive consequences. The resurrection of our German life was begun in these last twenty years, and particularly in the sacred year 1813, with a courage inspired by God. But now the house of our fathers is shaken from the summit to the base. Forward! let us raise it, new and fair, and such as the true temple of the true God should be.

"Small is the number of those who resist, and who wish to oppose themselves as a dyke against the torrent of the progress of higher humanity among the German people. Why should vast whole masses bow beneath the yoke of a perverse minority? And why, scarcely healed, should we fall back into a worse disease than that which we are leaving behind?

"Many of these seducers, and those are the most infamous, are playing the game of corruption with us; among them is Kotzebue, the most cunning and the worst of all, a real talking machine emitting all sorts of detestable speech and pernicious advice. His voice is skillful in removing from us all anger and bitterness against the most unjust measures, and is just such as kings require to put us to sleep again in that old hazy slumber which is the death of nations. Every day he odiously betrays his country, and nevertheless, despite his treason, remains an idol for half Germany, which, dazzled by him, accepts unresisting the poison poured out by him in his periodic pamphlets, wrapped up and protected as he is by the seductive mantle of a great poetic reputation. Incited by him, the princes of Germany, who have forgotten their promises, will allow nothing free or good to be accomplished; or if anything of the kind is accomplished in spite of them, they will league themselves with the French to annihilate it. That the history of our time may not be covered with eternal ignominy, it is necessary that he should fall.

"I have always said that if we wish to find a great and supreme remedy for the state of abasement in which we are, none must shrink from combat nor from suffering; and the real liberty of the German people will only be assured when the good citizen sets himself or some other stake upon the game, and when every true son of the country, prepared for the struggle for justice, despises the good things of this world, and only desires those celestial good things which death holds in charge.

"Who then will strike this miserable hireling, this venal traitor?

"I have long been waiting in fear, in prayer, and in tears—I who am not born for murder—for some other to be beforehand with me, to set me free, and suffer me to continue my way along the sweet and peaceful path that I had chosen for myself. Well, despite my prayers and my tears, he who should strike does not present himself; indeed, every man, like myself, has a right to count upon some other, and everyone thus counting, every hour's delay, but makes our state worse; far at any moment—and how deep a shame would that be for us! Kotzebue may leave Germany, unpunished, and go to devour in Russia the treasures for which he has exchanged his honour, his conscience, and his German name. Who can preserve us from this shame, if every man, if I myself, do not feel strength to make myself the chosen instrument of God's justice? Therefore, forward! It shall be I who will courageously rush upon him (do not be alarmed), on him, the loathsome seducer; it shall be I who will kill the traitor, so that his misguiding voice, being extinguished, shall cease to lead us astray from the lessons of history and from the Spirit of God. An irresistible and solemn duty impels me to this deed, ever since I have recognised to what high destinies the German; nation may attain during this century, and ever since I have come to know the dastard and hypocrite who alone prevents it from reaching them; for me, as for every German who seeks the public good, this desire has became a strict and binding necessity. May I, by this national vengeance, indicate to all upright and loyal consciences where the true danger lies, and save our vilified and calumniated societies from the imminent danger that threatens them! May I, in short, spread terror among the cowardly and wicked, and courage and faith among the good! Speeches and writings lead to nothing; only actions work.

"I will act, therefore; and though driven violently away from my fair dreams of the future, I am none the less full of trust in God; I even experience a celestial joy, now that, like the Hebrews when they sought the promised land, I see traced before me, through darkness and death, that road at the end of which I shall have paid my debt to my country.

"Farewell, then, faithful hearts: true, this early separation is hard; true, your hopes, like my wishes, are disappointed; but let us be consoled by the primary thought that we have done what the voice of our country called upon us to do; that, you knew, is the principle according to which I have always lived. You will doubtless say among yourselves, 'Yes, thanks to our sacrifices, he had learned to know life and to taste the joys of earth, and he seemed: deeply to love his native country and the humble estate to which he was called'. Alas, yes, that is true! Under your protection, and amid your numberless sacrifices, my native land and life had become profoundly dear to me. Yes, thanks to you, I have penetrated into the Eden of knowledge, and have lived the free life of thought; thanks to you, I have looked into history, and have then returned to my own conscience to attach myself to the solid pillars of faith in the Eternal.

"Yes, I was to pass gently through this life as a preacher of the gospel; yes, in my constancy to my calling I was to be sheltered from the storms of this existence. But would that suffice to avert the danger that threatens Germany? And you yourselves, in your infinite lave, should you not rather push me on to risk my life for the good of all? So many modern Greeks have fallen already to free their country from the yoke of the Turks, and have died almost without any result and without any hope; and yet thousands of fresh martyrs keep up their courage and are ready to fall in their turn; and should I, then, hesitate to die?

"That I do not recognise your love, or that your love is but a trifling consideration with me, you will not believe. What else should impel me to die if not my devotion to you and to Germany, and the need of proving this devotion to my family and my country?

"You, mother, will say, 'Why have I brought up a son

whom I loved and who loved me, for whom I have undergone a thousand cares and toils, who, thanks to my prayers and my example, was impressionable to good influences, and from whom, after my long and weary course, I hoped to receive attentions like those which I have given him? Why does he now abandon me?'

"Oh, my kind and tender mother! Yes, you will perhaps say that; but could not the mother of anyone else say the same, and everything go off thus in words when there is need to act for the country? And if no one would act, what would become of that mother of us all who is called Germany?

"But no; such complaints are far from you, you noble woman! I understood your appeal once before, and at this present hour, if no one came forward in the German cause, you yourself would urge me to the fight. I have two brothers and two sisters before me, all noble and loyal. They will remain to you, mother; and besides you will have for sons all the children of Germany who love their country.

"Every man has a destiny which he has to accomplish: mine is devoted to the action that I am about to undertake; if I were to live another fifty years, I could not live more happily than I have done lately. Farewell, mother: I commend you to the protection of God; may He raise you to that joy which misfortunes can no longer trouble! Take your grandchildren, to whom I should so much have liked to be a loving friend, to the top of our beautiful mountains soon. There, on that altar raised by the Lord Himself in the midst of Germany, let them devote themselves, swearing to take up the sword as soon as they have strength to lift it, and to lay it down only when our brethren are all united in liberty, when all Germans, having a liberal constitution; are great before the Lord, powerful against their neighbours, and united among themselves.

"May my country ever raise her happy gaze to Thee, Almighty Father! May Thy blessing fall abundantly upon her harvests ready to be cut and her armies ready for battle, and recognising the blessings that Thou host showered upon us, may the German nation ever be first among nations to rise and uphold the cause of humanity, which is Thy image upon earth!

"Your eternally attached son, brother and friend, "KARL-LUDWIG SAND. "JENA, the beginning of March, 1819."

Sand, who, as we have said, had at first been taken to the hospital, was removed at the end of three months to the prison at Mannheim, where the governor, Mr. G——, had caused a room to be prepared for him. There he remained two months longer in a state of extreme weakness: his left arm was completely paralysed; his voice was very weak; every movement gave him horrible pain, and thus it was not until the 11th of August—that is to say, five months after the event that we have narrated—that he was able to write to his family the following letter:—

"MY VERY DEAR PARENTS:—The grand-duke's commission of inquiry informed me yesterday that it might be possible I should have the intense joy of a visit from you, and that I might perhaps see you here and embrace you—you, mother, and some of my brothers and sisters.

"Without being surprised at this fresh proof of your motherly love, I have felt an ardent remembrance reawaken of the happy life that we spent gently together. Joy and grief, desire and sacrifice, agitate my heart violently, and I have had to weigh these various impulses one against the other, and with the force of reason, in order to resume mastery of myself and to take a decision in regard to my wishes.

"The balance has inclined in the direction of sacrifice.

"You know, mother, how much joy and courage a look from your eyes, daily intercourse with you, and your pious and high-minded conversation, might bring me during my very short time. But you also know my position, and you are too well acquainted with the natural course of all these painful inquiries, not to feel as I do, that such annoyance, continually recurring, would greatly trouble the pleasure of our companionship, if it did not indeed succeed in entirely destroying it. Then, mother, after the long and fatiguing journey that you would be obliged to make in order to see me, think of the terrible sorrow of the farewell when the moment came to part in this world. Let us therefore abide by the sacrifice, according to God's will, and let us yield ourselves only to that sweet community of thought which distance cannot interrupt, in which I find my only joys, and which, in spite of men, will always be granted us by the Lord, our Father.

"As for my physical state, I knew nothing about it. You see, however, since at last I am writing to you myself, that I have come past my first uncertainties. As for the rest, I know too little of the structure of my own body to give any opinion as to what my wounds may determine for it. Except that a little strength has returned to me, its state is still the same, and I endure it calmly and patiently; for God comes to my help, and gives me courage and firmness. He will help me, believe me, to find all the joys of the soul and to be strong in mind. Amen.

"May you live happy!—Your deeply respectful son, "KARL-LUDWIG SAND."

A month after this letter came tender answers from all the family. We will quote only that of Sand's mother, because it completes the idea which the reader may have formed already of this great-hearted woman, as her son always calls her.

"DEAR, INEXPRESSIBLY DEAR KARL,—How Sweet it was to me to see the writing of your beloved hand after so long a time! No journey would have been so painful and no road so long as to prevent me from coming to you, and I would go, in deep and infinite love, to any end of the earth in the mere hope of catching sight of you.

"But, as I well know both your tender affection and your profound anxiety for me, and as you give me, so firmly and upon such manly reflection, reasons against which I can say nothing, and which I can but honour, it shall be, my well-beloved Karl, as you have wished and decided. We will continue, without speech, to communicate our thoughts; but be satisfied, nothing can separate us; I enfold you in my soul, and my material thoughts watch over you.

"May this infinite love which upholds us, strengthens us, and leads us all to a better life, preserve, dear Karl, your courage and firmness.

"Farewell, and be invariably assured that I shall never cease to love you strongly and deeply.

"Your faithful mother, who loves you to eternity."

Sand replied:—

January 1820, from my isle of Patmos. "MY DEAR PARENTS, BROTHERS, AND SISTERS,—

"In the middle of the month of September last year I received, through the grand-duke's special commission of inquiry, whose humanity you have already appreciated, your dear letters of the end of August and the beginning of September, which had such magical influence that they inundated me with joy by transporting me into the inmost circle of your hearts.

"You, my tender father, you write to me on the sixty-seventh anniversary of your birth, and you bless me by the outpouring of your most tender love.

"You, my well-beloved mother, you deign to promise the continuance of your maternal affection, in which I have at all times constantly believed; and thus I have received the blessings of both of you, which, in my present position, will exercise a more beneficent influence upon me than any of the things that all the kings of the earth, united together, could grant me. Yes, you strengthen me abundantly by your blessed love, and I render thanks to you, my beloved parents, with that respectful submission that my heart will always inculcate as the first duty of a son.

"But the greater your love and the more affectionate your letters, the more do I suffer, I must acknowledge, from the voluntary sacrifice that we have imposed upon ourselves in not seeing one another; and the only reason, my dear parents, why I have delayed to reply to you, was to give myself time to recover the strength which I have lost.

"You too, dear brother-in-law and dear sister, assure me of your sincere and uninterrupted attachment. And yet, after the fright that I have spread among you all, you seem not to know exactly what to think of me; but my heart, full of gratitude for your past kindness, comforts itself; for your actions speak and tell me that, even if you wished no longer to love me as I love you, you would not be able to do otherwise. These actions mean more to me at this hour than any possible protestations, nay, than even the tenderest words.

"And you also, my kind brother, you would have consented to hurry with our beloved mother to the shores of the Rhine, to this place where the real links of the soul were welded between us, where we were doubly brothers; but tell me, are you not really here, in thought and in spirit, when I consider the rich fountain of consolation brought me by your cordial and tender letter?

"And, you, kind sister-in-law, as you showed yourself from the first, in your delicate tenderness, a true sister, so I find you again at present. There are still the same tender relations, still the same sisterly affection; your consolations, which emanate from a deep and submissive piety, have fallen refreshingly into the depths of my heart. But, dear sister-in-law, I must tell you, as well as the others, that you are too liberal towards me in dispensing your esteem and praises, and your exaggeration has cast me back face to face with my inmost judge, who has shown me in the mirror of my conscience the image of my every weakness.

"You, kind Julia, you desire nothing else but to save me from the fate that awaits me; and you assure me in your own name and in that of you all, that you, like the others, would rejoice to endure it in my place; in that I recognise you fully, and I recognise, too, those sweet and tender relations in which we have been brought up from childhood. Oh, be comforted, dear Julia; thanks to the protection of God, I promise you: that it will be easy for me, much easier than I should have thought, to bear what falls to my lot. Receive, then, all of you, my warm and sincere thanks for having thus rejoiced my heart.

"Now that I know from these strengthening letters that, like the prodigal son, the love and goodness of my family are greater on my return than at my departure, I will, as carefully as possible, paint for you my physical and moral state, and I pray God to supplement my words by His strength, so that my letter may contain an equivalent of what yours brought to me, and may help you to reach that state of calm and serenity to which I have myself attained.

"Hardened, by having gained power over myself, against the good and ill of this earth, you knew already that of late years I have lived only for moral joys, and I must say that, touched by my efforts, doubtless, the Lord, who is the sacred fount of all that is good, has rendered me apt in seeking them and in tasting them to the full. God is ever near me, as formerly, and I find in Him the sovereign principle of the creation of all things; in Him, our holy Father, not only consolation and strength, but an unalterable Friend, full of the holiest love, who will accompany me in all places where I may need His consolations. Assuredly, if He had turned from me, or if I had turned away my eyes from Him, I should now find myself very unfortunate and wretched; but by His grace, on the contrary, lowly and weak creature as I am, He makes me strong and powerful against whatever can befall me.

"What I have hitherto revered as sacred, what I have desired as good what I have aspired to as heavenly, has in no respect changed now. And I thank God for it, for I should now be in great despair if I were compelled to recognise that my heart had adored deceptive images and enwrapped itself in fugitive chimeras. Thus my faith in these ideas and my pure love far them, guardian angels of my spirit as they are, increase moment by moment, and will go on increasing to my end, and I hope that I may pass all the more easily from this world into eternity. I pass my silent life in Christian exaltation and humility, and I sometimes have those visions from above through which I have, from my birth, adored heaven upon earth, and which give me power to raise myself to the Lord upon the eager wings of my prayers. My illness, though long, painful, and cruel, has always been sufficiently mastered by my will to let me busy myself to some result with history, positive sciences, and the finer parts of religious education, and when my suffering became more violent and for a time interrupted these occupations, I struggled successfully, nevertheless, against ennui; for the memories of the past, my resignation to the present, and my faith in the future were rich enough and strong enough in me and round me to prevent my falling from my terrestrial paradise. According to my principles, I would never, in the position in which I am and in which I have placed myself, have been willing to ask anything for my own comfort; but so much kindness and care have been lavished upon me, with so much delicacy and humanity,—which alas! I am unable to return—by every person with whom I have been brought into contact, that wishes which I should not have dared to frame in the mast private recesses of my heart have been more than exceeded. I have never been so much overcome by bodily pains that I could not say within myself, while I lifted my thoughts to heaven, 'Come what may of this ray.' And great as these gains have been, I could not dream of comparing them with those sufferings of the soul that we feel so profoundly and poignantly in the recognition of our weaknesses and faults.

"Moreover, these pains seldom now cause me to lose consciousness; the swelling and inflammation never made great headway, and the fever has always been moderate, though for nearly ten months I have been forced to remain lying on my back, unable to raise myself, and although more than forty pints of matter have come from my chest at the place where the heart is. No, an the contrary, the wound, though still open, is in a good state; and I owe that not only to the excellent nursing around me, but also to the pure blood that I received from you, my mother. Thus I have lacked neither earthly assistance nor heavenly encouragement. Thus, on the anniversary of my birth, I had every reason—oh, not to curse the hour in which I was born, but, on the contrary, after serious contemplation of the world, to thank God and you, my dear parents, for the life that you have given me! I celebrated it, on the 18th of October, by a peaceful and ardent submission to the holy will of God. On Christmas Day I tried to put myself into the temper of children who are devoted to the Lord; and with God's help the new year will pass like its predecessor, in bodily pain, perhaps, but certainly in spiritual joy. And with this wish, the only one that I form, I address myself to you, my dear parents, and to you and yours, my dear brothers and sisters.

"I cannot hope to see a twenty-fifth new year; so may the prayer that I have just made be granted! May this picture of my present state afford you some tranquillity, and may this letter that I write to you from the depths of my heart not only prove to you that I am not unworthy of the inexpressible love that you all display, but, on the contrary, ensure this love to me for eternity.

"Within the last few days I have also received your dear letter of the 2nd of December, my kind mother, and the grind-duke's commission has deigned to let me also read my kind brother's letter which accompanied yours. You give me the best of news in regard to the health of all of you, and send me preserved fruits from our dear home. I thank you for them from the bottom of my heart. What causes me most joy in the matter is that you have been solicitously busy about me in summer as in winter, and that you and my dear Julia gathered them and prepared them for me at home, and I abandon my whole soul to that sweet enjoyment.

"I rejoice sincerely at my little cousin's coming into the world; I joyfully congratulate the good parents and the grandparents; I transport myself, for his baptism, into that beloved parish, where I offer him my affection as his Christian brother, and call down on him all the blessings of heaven.

"We shall be obliged, I think, to give up this correspondence, so as not to inconvenience the grand-duke's commission. I finish, therefore, by assuring you, once more, but for the last time, perhaps, of my profound filial submission and of my fraternal affection.—Your most tenderly attached "KARL-LUDWIG SAND."

Indeed, from that moment all correspondence between Karl and his family ceased, and he only wrote to them, when he knew his fate, one more letter, which we shall see later on.

We have seen by what attentions Sand was surrounded; their humanity never flagged for an instant. It is the truth, too, that no one saw in him an ordinary murderer, that many pitied him under their breath, and that some excused him aloud. The very commission appointed by the grand-duke prolonged the affair as much as possible; for the severity of Sand's wounds had at first given rise to the belief that there would be no need of calling in the executioner, and the commission was well pleased that God should have undertaken the execution of the judgment. But these expectations were deceived: the skill of the doctor defeated, not indeed the wound, but death: Sand did not recover, but he remained alive; and it began to be evident that it would be needful to kill him.

Indeed, the Emperor Alexander, who had appointed Kotzebue his councillor, and who was under no misapprehension as to the cause of the murder, urgently demanded that justice should take its course. The commission of inquiry was therefore obliged to set to work; but as its members were sincerely desirous of having some pretext to delay their proceedings, they ordered that a physician from Heidelberg should visit Sand and make an exact report upon his case; as Sand was kept lying down and as he could not be executed in his bed, they hoped that the physician's report, by declaring it impossible for the prisoner to rise, would come to their assistance and necessitate a further respite.

The chosen doctor came accordingly to Mannheim, and introducing himself to Sand as though attracted by the interest that he inspired, asked him whether he did not feel somewhat better, and whether it would be impossible to rise. Sand looked at him for an instant, and then said, with a smile—

"I understand, sir; they wish to know whether I am strong enough to mount a scaffold: I know nothing about it myself, but we will make the experiment together."

With these words he rose, and accomplishing, with superhuman courage, what he had not attempted for fourteen months, walked twice round the room, came back to his bed, upon which he seated himself, and said:

"You see, sir, I am strong enough; it would therefore be wasting precious time to keep my judges longer about my affair; so let them deliver their judgment, for nothing now prevents its execution."

The doctor made his report; there was no way of retreat; Russia was becoming more and more pressing, and an the 5th of May 1820 the high court of justice delivered the following judgment, which was confirmed on the 12th by His Royal Highness the Grand-Duke of Baden:

"In the matters under investigation and after administration of the interrogatory and hearing the defences, and considering the united opinions of the court of justice at Mannheim and the further consultations of the court of justice which declare the accused, Karl Sand of Wonsiedel, guilty of murder, even on his own confession, upon the person of the Russian imperial Councillor of State, Kotzebue; it is ordered accordingly, for his just punishment and for an example that may deter other people, that he is to be put from life to death by the sword.

"All the costs of these investigations, including these occasioned by his public execution, will be defrayed from the funds of the law department, on account of his want of means."

We see that, though it condemned the accused to death, which indeed could hardly be avoided, the sentence was both in form and substance as mild as possible, since, though Sand was convicted, his poor family was not reduced by the expenses of a long and costly trial to complete ruin.

Five days were still allowed to elapse, and the verdict was not announced until the 17th. When Sand was informed that two councillors of justice were at the door, he guessed that they were coming to read his sentence to him; he asked a moment to rise, which he had done but once before, in the instance already narrated, during fourteen months. And indeed he was so weak that he could not stand to hear the sentence, and after having greeted the deputation that death sent to him, he asked to sit down, saying that he did so not from cowardice of soul but from weakness of body; then he added, "You are welcome, gentlemen; far I have suffered so much for fourteen months past that you come to me as angels of deliverance."

He heard the sentence quite unaffectedly and with a gentle smile upon his lips; then, when the reading was finished, he said—

"I look for no better fate, gentlemen, and when, more than a year ago, I paused on the little hill that overlooks the town, I saw beforehand the place where my grave would be; and so I ought to thank God and man far having prolonged my existence up to to-day."

The councillors withdrew; Sand stood up a second time to greet them on their departure, as he had done on their entrance; then he sat down again pensively in his chair, by which Mr. G, the governor of the prison, was standing. After a moment of silence, a tear appeared at each of the condemned man's eyelids, and ran down his cheeks; then, turning suddenly to Mr. G——, whom he liked very much, he said, "I hope that my parents would rather see me die by this violent death than of some slow and shameful disease. As for me, I am glad that I shall soon hear the hour strike in which my death will satisfy those who hate me, and those wham, according to my principles, I ought to hate."

Then he wrote to his family.

"MANNHEIM

"17th of the month of spring, 1820

"DEAR PARENTS, BROTHERS, AND SISTERS,— You should have received my last letters through the grand-duke's commission; in them I answered yours, and tried to console you for my position by describing the state of my soul as it is, the contempt to which I have attained for everything fragile and earthly, and by which one must necessarily be overcome when such matters are weighed against the fulfilment of an idea, or that intellectual liberty which alone can nourish the soul; in a word, I tried to console you by the assurance that the feelings, principles, and convictions of which I formerly spoke are faithfully preserved in me and have remained exactly the same; but I am sure all this was an unnecessary precaution on my part, for there was never a time when you asked anything else of me than to have God before my eyes and in my heart; and you have seen how, under your guidance, this precept so passed into my soul that it became my sole object of happiness for this world and the next; no doubt, as He was in and near me, God will be in and near you at the moment when this letter brings you the news of my sentence. I die willingly, and the Lord will give me strength to die as one ought to die.

"I write to you perfectly quiet and calm about all things, and I hope that your lives too will pass calmly and tranquilly until the moment when our souls meet again full of fresh force to love one another and to share eternal happiness together.

"As for me, such as I have lived as long as I have known myself—that is to say, in a serenity full of celestial desires and a courageous and indefatigable love of liberty, such I am about to die.

"May God be with you and with me!—Your son, brother, and friend, "KARL-LUDWIG SAND."

From that moment his serenity remained un troubled; during the whole day he talked more gaily than usual, slept well, did not awake until half-past seven, said that he felt stronger, and thanked God for visiting him thus.

The nature of the verdict had been known since the day before, and it had been learned that the execution was fixed for the 20th of May—that is to say, three full days after the sentence had been read to the accused.

Henceforward, with Sand's permission, persons who wished to speak to him and whom he was not reluctant to see, were admitted: three among these paid him long and noteworthy visits.

One was Major Holzungen, of the Baden army, who was

in command of the patrol that had arrested him, or rather picked him up, dying, and carried him to the hospital. He asked him whether he recognised him, and Sand's head was so clear when he stabbed himself, that although he saw the major only for a moment and had never seen him again since, he remembered the minutest details of the costume which he had been wearing fourteen months previously, and which was the full-dress uniform. When the talk fell upon the death to which Sand was to submit at so early an age, the major pitied him; but Sand answered, with a smile, "There is only one difference between you and me, major; it is that I shall die far my convictions, and you will die for someone else's convictions."

After the major came a young student from Jena whom Sand had known at the university. He happened to be in the duchy of Baden and wished to visit him. Their recognition was touching, and the student wept much; but Sand consoled him with his usual calmness and serenity.

Then a workman asked to be admitted to see Sand, on the plea that he had been his schoolfellow at Wonsiedel, and although he did not remember his name, he ordered him to be let in: the workman reminded him that he had been one of the little army that Sand had commanded on the day of the assault of St. Catherine's tower. This indication guided Sand, who recognised him perfectly, and then spoke with tender affection of his native place and his dear mountains. He further charged him to greet his family, and to beg his mother, father, brothers, and sisters once more not to be grieved on his account, since the messenger who undertook to deliver his last wards could testify in how calm and joyful a temper he was awaiting death.

To this workman succeeded one of the guests whom Sand had met on the staircase directly after Kotzebue's death. He asked him whether he acknowledged his crime and whether he felt any repentance. Sand replied, "I had thought about it during a whole year. I have been thinking of it for fourteen months, and my opinion has never varied in any respect: I did what I should have done."

After the departure of this last visitor, Sand sent for Mr. G——, the governor of the prison, and told him that he should like to talk to the executioner before the execution, since he wished to ask for instructions as to how he should hold himself so as to render the operation most certain and easy. Mr. G—— made some objections, but Sand insisted with his usual gentleness, and Mr. G—— at last promised that the man in question should be asked to call at the prison as soon as he arrived from Heidelberg, where he lived.

The rest of the day was spent in seeing more visitors and in philosophical and moral talks, in which Sand developed his social and religious theories with a lucidity of expression and an elevation of thought such as he had, perhaps, never before shown. The governor of the prison from whom I heard these details, told me that he should all his life regret that he did not know shorthand, so that he might have noted all these thoughts, which would have formed a pendant to the Phaedo.

Night came. Sand spent part of the evening writing; it is thought that he was composing a poem; but no doubt he burned it, for no trace of it was found. At eleven he went to bed, and slept until six in the morning. Next day he bore the dressing of his wound, which was always very painful, with extraordinary courage, without fainting, as he sometimes did, and without suffering a single complaint to escape him: he had spoken the truth; in the presence of death God gave him the grace of allowing his strength to return. The operation was over; Sand was lying down as usual, and Mr. G——was sitting on the foot of his bed, when the door opened and a man came in and bowed to Sand and to Mr. G——. The governor of the prison immediately stood up, and said to Sand in a voice the emotion of which he could not conceal, "The person who is bowing to you is Mr. Widemann of Heidelberg, to whom you wished to speak."

Then Sand's face was lighted up by a strange joy; he sat up and said, "Sir, you are welcome." Then, making his visitor sit down by his bed, and taking his hand, he began to thank him for being so obliging, and spoke in so intense a tone and so gentle a voice, that Mr. Widemann, deeply moved, could not answer. Sand encouraged him to speak and to give him the details for which he wished, and in order to reassure him, said, "Be firm, sir; for I, on my part, will not fail you: I will not move; and even if you should need two or three strokes to separate my head from my body, as I am told is sometimes the case, do not be troubled on that account."

Then Sand rose, leaning on Mr. G——, to go through

with the executioner the strange and terrible rehearsal of the drama in which he was to play the leading part on the morrow. Mr. Widemann made him sit in a chair and take the required position, and went into all the details of the execution with him. Then Sand, perfectly instructed, begged him not to hurry and to take his time. Then he thanked him beforehand; "for," added he, "afterwards I shall not be able." Then Sand returned to his bed, leaving the executioner paler and more trembling than himself. All these details have been preserved by Mr. G——; for as to the executioner, his emotion was so great that he could remember nothing.

After Mr. Widemann, three clergymen were introduced, with whom Sand conversed upon religious matters: one of them stayed six hours with him, and on leaving him told him that he was commissioned to obtain from him a promise of not speaking to the people at the place of execution. Sand gave the promise, and added, "Even if I desired to do so, my voice has become so weak that people could not hear it."

Meanwhile the scaffold was being erected in the meadow that extends on the left of the road to Heidelberg. It was a platform five to six feet high and ten feet wide each way. As it was expected that, thanks to the interest inspired by the prisoner and to the nearness to Whitsuntide, the crowd would be immense, and as some movement from the universities was apprehended, the prison guards had been trebled, and General Neustein had been ordered to Mannheim from Carlsruhe, with twelve hundred infantry, three hundred and fifty cavalry, and a company of artillery with guns.

On, the afternoon of the 19th there arrived, as had been foreseen, so many students, who took up their abode in the neighbouring villages, that it was decided to put forward the hour of the execution, and to let it take place at five in the morning instead of at eleven, as had been arranged. But Sand's consent was necessary for this; for he could not be executed until three full days after the reading of his sentence, and as the sentence had not been read to him till half-past ten Sand had a right to live till eleven o'clock.

Before four in the morning the officials went into the condemned man's room; he was sleeping so soundly that they were obliged to awaken him. He opened his eyes with a smile, as was his custom, and guessing why they came, asked, "Can I have slept so well that it is already eleven in the morning?" They told him that it was not, but that they had come to ask his permission to put forward the time; for, they told him, same collision between the students and the soldiers was feared, and as the military preparations were very thorough, such a collision could not be otherwise than fatal to his friends. Sand answered that he was ready that very moment, and only asked time enough to take a bath, as the ancients were accustomed to do before going into battle. But as the verbal authorisation which he had given was not sufficient, a pen and paper were given to Sand, and he wrote, with a steady hand and in his usual writing:

"I thank the authorities of Mannheim for anticipating my most eager wishes by making my execution six hours earlier.

"Sit nomen Domini benedictum.

"From the prison room, May 20th, day of my deliverance.
"KARL-LUDWIG SAND."

When Sand had given these two lines to the recorder, the physician came to him to dress his wound, as usual. Sand looked at him with a smile, and then asked, "Is it really worth the trouble?"

"You will be stronger for it," answered the physician.

"Then do it," said Sand.

A bath was brought. Sand lay down in it, and had his long and beautiful hair arranged with the greatest care; then his toilet being completed, he put on a frock-coat of the German shape—that is to say, short and with the shirt collar turned back aver the shoulders, close white trousers, and high boots. Then Sand seated himself on his bed and prayed some time in a low voice with the clergy; then, when he had finished, he said these two lines of Korner's:

"All that is earthly is ended,
  And the life of heaven begins."

He next took leave of the physician and the priests, saying to them, "Do not attribute the emotion of my voice to weakness but to gratitude." Then, upon these gentlemen offering to accompany him to the scaffold, he said, "There is no need; I am perfectly prepared, at peace with God and with my conscience. Besides, am I not almost a Churchman myself?" And when one of them asked whether he was not going out of life in a spirit of hatred, he returned, "Why, good heavens! have I ever felt any?"

An increasing noise was audible from the street, and Sand said again that he was at their disposal and that he was ready. At this moment the executioner came in with his two assistants; he was dressed in a long wadded black coat, beneath which he hid his sword. Sand offered him his hand affectionately; and as Mr. Widemann, embarrassed by the sword which he wished to keep Sand from seeing, did not venture to come forward, Sand said to him, "Come along and show me your sword; I have never seen one of the kind, and am curious to know what it is like."

Mr. Widemann, pale and trembling, presented the weapon to him; Sand examined it attentively, and tried the edge with his finger.

"Come," said he, "the blade is good; do not tremble, and all will go well." Then, turning to Mr. G——, who was weeping, he said to him, "You will be good enough, will you not, to do me the service of leading me to the scaffold?"

Mr. G——made a sign of assent with his head, for he could not answer. Sand took his arm, and spoke for the third time, saying once more, "Well, what are you waiting for, gentlemen? I am ready."

When they reached the courtyard, Sand saw all the prisoners weeping at their windows. Although he had never seen them, they were old friends of his; for every time they passed his door, knowing that the student who had killed Kotzebue lay within, they used to lift their chain, that he might not be disturbed by the noise.

All Mannheim was in the streets that led to the place of

execution, and many patrols were passing up and down. On the day when the sentence was announced the whole town had been sought through for a chaise in which to convey Sand to the scaffold, but no one, not even the coach-builders, would either let one out or sell one; and it had been necessary, therefore, to buy one at Heidelberg without saying for what purpose.

Sand found this chaise in the courtyard, and got into it with Mr. G——. Turning to him, he whispered in his ear, "Sir, if you see me turn pale, speak my name to me, my name only, do you hear? That will be enough."

The prison gate was opened, and Sand was seen; then every voice cried with one impulse, "Farewell, Sand, farewell!"

And at the same time flowers, some of which fell into the carriage, were thrown by the crowd that thronged the street, and from the windows. At these friendly cries and at this spectacle, Sand, who until then had shown no moment of weakness, felt tears rising in spite of himself, and while he returned the greetings made to him on all sides, he murmured in a low voice, "O my God, give me courage!"

This first outburst over, the procession set out amid deep silence; only now and again same single voice would call out, "Farewell, Sand!" and a handkerchief waved by some hand that rose out of the crowd would show from what paint the last call came. On each side of the chaise walked two of the prison officials, and behind the chaise came a second conveyance with the municipal authorities.

The air was very cold: it had rained all night, and the

dark and cloudy sky seemed to share in the general sadness. Sand, too weak to remain sitting up, was half lying upon the shoulder of Mr. G——-, his companion; his face was gentle, calm and full of pain; his brow free and open, his features, interesting though without regular beauty, seemed to have aged by several years during the fourteen months of suffering that had just elapsed. The chaise at last reached the place of execution, which was surrounded by a battalion of infantry; Sand lowered his eyes from heaven to earth and saw the scaffold. At this sight he smiled gently, and as he left the carriage he said, "Well, God has given me strength so far."

The governor of the prison and the chief officials lifted him that he might go up the steps. During that short ascent pain kept him bowed, but when he had reached the top he stood erect again, saying, "Here then is the place where I am to die!"

Then before he came to the chair on which he was to be seated for the execution, he turned his eyes towards Mannheim, and his gaze travelled over all the throng that surrounded him; at that moment a ray of sunshine broke through the clouds. Sand greeted it with a smile and sat down.

Then, as, according to the orders given, his sentence was to be read to him a second time, he was asked whether he felt strong enough to hear it standing. Sand answered that he would try, and that if his physical strength failed him, his moral strength would uphold him. He rose immediately from the fatal chair, begging Mr. G——to stand near enough to support him if he should chance to stagger. The precaution was unnecessary, Sand did not stagger.

After the judgment had been read, he sat down again and said in a laud voice, "I die trusting in God."

But at these words Mr. G———interrupted him.

"Sand," said he, "what did you promise?"

"True," he answered; "I had forgotten." He was silent, therefore, to the crowd; but, raising his right hand and extending it solemnly in the air, he said in a low voice, so that he might be heard only by those who were around him, "I take God to witness that I die for the freedom of Germany."

Then, with these words, he did as Conradin did with his glove; he threw his rolled-up handkerchief over the line of soldiers around him, into the midst of the people.

Then the executioner came to cut off his hair; but Sand at first objected.

"It is for your mother," said Mr. Widemann.

"On your honour, sir?" asked Sand.

"On my honour."

"Then do it," said Sand, offering his hair to the executioner.

Only a few curls were cut off, those only which fell at the back, the others were tied with a ribbon on the top of the head. The executioner then tied his hands on his breast, but as that position was oppressive to him and compelled him an account of his wound to bend his head, his hands were laid flat on his thighs and fixed in that position with ropes. Then, when his eyes were about to be bound, he begged Mr. Widemann to place the bandage in such a manner that he could see the light to his last moment. His wish was fulfilled.

Then a profound and mortal stillness hovered over the whole crowd and surrounded the scaffold. The executioner drew his sword, which flashed like lightning and fell. Instantly a terrible cry rose at once from twenty thousand bosoms; the head had not fallen, and though it had sunk towards the breast still held to the neck. The executioner struck a second time, and struck off at the same blow the head and a part of the hand.

In the same moment, notwithstanding the efforts of the soldiers, their line was broken through; men and women rushed upon the scaffold, the blood was wiped up to the last drop with handkerchiefs; the chair upon which Sand had sat was broken and divided into pieces, and those who could not obtain one, cut fragments of bloodstained wood from the scaffold itself.

The head and body were placed in a coffin draped with black, and carried back, with a large military escort, to the prison. At midnight the body was borne silently, without torches or lights, to the Protestant cemetery, in which Kotzebue had been buried fourteen months previously. A grave had been mysteriously dug; the coffin was lowered into it, and those who were present at the burial were sworn upon the New Testament not to reveal the spot where Sand was buried until such time as they were freed from their oath. Then the grave was covered again with the turf, that had been skilfully taken off, and that was relaid on the same spat, so that no new grave could be perceived; then the nocturnal gravediggers departed, leaving guards at the entrance.

There, twenty paces apart, Sand and Kotzebue rest: Kotzebue opposite the gate in the most conspicuous spot of the cemetery, and beneath a tomb upon which is engraved this inscription:

"The world persecuted him without pity, Calumny was his sad portion, He found no happiness save in the arms of his wife, And no repose save in the bosom of death. Envy dogged him to cover his path with thorns, Love bade his roses blossom; May Heaven pardon him As he pardons earth!"

In contrast with this tall and showy monument, standing, as we have said, in the most conspicuous spot of the cemetery, Sand's grave must be looked far in the corner to the extreme left of the entrance gate; and a wild plum tree, some leaves of which every passing traveller carries away, rises alone upon the grave, which is devoid of any inscription.

As far the meadow in which Sand was executed, it is still called by the people "Sand's Himmelsfartsweise," which signifies "The manner of Sand's ascension."

Toward the end of September, 1838, we were at Mannheim, where I had stayed three days in order to collect all the details I could find about the life and death of Karl-Ludwig Sand. But at the end of these three days, in spite of my active investigations, these details still remained extremely incomplete, either because I applied in the wrong quarters, or because, being a foreigner, I inspired same distrust in those to whom I applied. I was leaving Mannheim, therefore, somewhat disappointed, and after having visited the little

Protestant cemetery where Sand and Kotzebue are buried at twenty paces from each other, I had ordered my driver to take the road to Heidelberg, when, after going a few yards, he, who knew the object of my inquiries, stopped of himself and asked me whether I should not like to see the place where Sand was executed. At the same time he pointed to a little mound situated in the middle of a meadow and a few steps from a brook. I assented eagerly, and although the driver remained on the highroad with my travelling companions, I soon recognised the spot indicated, by means of some relics of cypress branches, immortelles, and forget-me-nots scattered upon the earth. It will readily be understood that this sight, instead of diminishing my desire for information, increased it. I was feeling, then, more than ever dissatisfied at going away, knowing so little, when I saw a man of some five-and-forty to fifty years old, who was walking a little distance from the place where I myself was, and who, guessing the cause that drew me thither, was looking at me with curiosity. I determined to make a last effort, and going up to him, I said, "Oh, sir, I am a stranger; I am travelling to collect all the rich and poetic traditions of your Germany. By the way in which you look at me, I guess that you know which of them attracts me to this meadow. Could you give me any information about the life and death of Sand?"

"With what object, sir?" the person to whom I spoke asked me in almost unintelligible French.

"With a very German object, be assured, sir," I replied. "From the little I have learned, Sand seems to me to be one of those ghosts that appear only the greater and the more poetic for being wrapped in a shroud stained with blood. But he is not known in France; he might be put on the same level there with a Fieschi or a Meunier, and I wish, to the best of my ability, to enlighten the minds of my countrymen about him."

"It would be a great pleasure to me, sir, to assist in such an undertaking; but you see that I can scarcely speak French; you do not speak German at all; so that we shall find it difficult to understand each other."

"If that is all," I returned, "I have in my carriage yonder an interpreter, or rather an interpretress, with whom you will, I hope, be quite satisfied, who speaks German like Goethe, and to whom, when you have once begun to speak to her, I defy you not to tell everything."

"Let us go, then, sir," answered the pedestrian. "I ask no better than to be agreeable to you."

We walked toward the carriage, which was still waiting on the highroad, and I presented to my travelling companion the new recruit whom I had just gained. The usual greetings were exchanged, and the dialogue began in the purest Saxon. Though I did not understand a word that was said, it was easy for me to see, by the rapidity of the questions and the length of the answers, that the conversation was most interesting. At last, at the end of half an hours growing desirous of knowing to what point they had come, I said, "Well?"

"Well," answered my interpreter, "you are in luck's way, and you could not have asked a better person."

"The gentleman knew Sand, then?"

"The gentleman is the governor of the prison in which Sand was confined."

"Indeed?"

"For nine months—that is to say, from the day he left the hospital— this gentleman saw him every day."

"Excellent!"

"But that is not all: this gentleman was with him in the carriage that took him to execution; this gentleman was with him on the scaffold; there's only one portrait of Sand in all Mannheim, and this gentleman has it."

I was devouring every word; a mental alchemist, I was opening my crucible and finding gold in it.

"Just ask," I resumed eagerly, "whether the gentleman will allow us to take down in writing the particulars that he can give me."

My interpreter put another question, then, turning towards me, said, "Granted."

Mr. G——got into the carriage with us, and instead of going on to Heidelberg, we returned to Mannheim, and alighted at the prison.

Mr. G—-did not once depart from the ready kindness that he had shown. In the most obliging manner, patient over the minutest trifles, and remembering most happily, he went over every circumstance, putting himself at my disposal like a professional guide. At last, when every particular about Sand had been sucked dry, I began to ask him about the manner in which executions were performed. "As to that," said he, "I can offer you an introduction to someone at Heidelberg who can give you all the information you can wish for upon the subject."

I accepted gratefully, and as I was taking leave of Mr. G——, after thanking him a thousand times, he handed me the offered letter. It bore this superscription: "To Herr-doctor Widemann, No. III High Street, Heidelberg."

I turned to Mr. G—— once more.

"Is he, by chance, a relation of the man who executed Sand?" I asked.

"He is his son, and was standing by when the head fell.".

"What is his calling, then?"

"The same as that of his father, whom he succeeded."

"But you call him 'doctor'?"

"Certainly; with us, executioners have that title."

"But, then, doctors of what?"

"Of surgery."

"Really?" said I. "With us it is just the contrary; surgeons are called executioners."

"You will find him, moreover," added Mr. G——, "a very distinguished young man, who, although he was very young at that time, has retained a vivid recollection of that event. As for his poor father, I think he would as willingly have cut off his own right hand as have executed Sand; but if he had refused, someone else would have been found. So he had to do what he was ordered to do, and he did his best."

I thanked Mr. G——, fully resolving to make use of his letter, and we left for Heidelberg, where we arrived at eleven in the evening.

My first visit next day was to Dr. Widernann. It was not without some emotion, which, moreover, I saw reflected upon, the faces of my travelling companions, that I rang at the door of the last judge, as the Germans call him. An old woman opened the door to us, and ushered us into a pretty little study, on the left of a passage and at the foot of a staircase, where we waited while Mr. Widemann finished dressing. This little room was full of curiosities, madrepores, shells, stuffed birds, and dried plants; a double-barrelled gun, a powder-flask, and a game-bag showed that Mr. Widemann was a hunter.

After a moment we heard his footstep, and the door opened. Mr. Widemann was a very handsome young man, of thirty or thirty-two, with black whiskers entirely surrounding his manly and expressive face; his morning dress showed a certain rural elegance. He seemed at first not only embarrassed but pained by our visit. The aimless curiosity of which he seemed to be the object was indeed odd. I hastened to give him Mr. G——'s letter and to tell him what reason brought me. Then he gradually recovered himself, and at last showed himself no less hospitable and obliging towards us than he to whom we owed the introduction had been, the day before.

Mr. Widemann then gathered together all his remembrances; he, too, had retained a vivid recollection of Sand, and he told us among other things that his father, at the risk of bringing himself into ill odour, had asked leave to have a new scaffold made at his own expense, so that no other criminal might be executed upon the altar of the martyr's death. Permission had been given, and Mr. Widemann had used the wood of the scaffold for the doors and windows of a little country house standing in a vineyard. Then for three or four years this cottage became a shrine for pilgrims; but after a time, little by little, the crowd grew less, and at the present day, when some of those who wiped the blood from the scaffold with their handkerchiefs have became public functionaries, receiving salaries from Government, only foreigners ask, now and again, to see these strange relics.

Mr. Widemann gave me a guide; for, after hearing everything, I wanted to see everything. The house stands half a league away from Heidelberg, on the left of the road to Carlsruhe, and half-way up the mountain-side. It is perhaps the only monument of the kind that exists in the world.

Our readers will judge better from this anecdote than from anything more we could say, what sort of man he was who left such a memory in the hearts of his gaoler and his executioner.

www.ingramcontent.com/pod-product-compliance
Lightning Source LLC
LaVergne TN
LVHW041549070426
835507LV00011B/1004